ICE

ALISON MILFORD

WOW! facts

Badger Publishing Limited
Oldmedow Road,
Hardwick Industrial Estate,
King's Lynn PE30 4JJ
Telephone: 01438 791037

www.badgerlearning.co.uk

2 4 6 8 10 9 7 5 3 1

Ice ISBN 978-1-78464-012-5

Publisher: Susan Ross
Senior Editor: Danny Pearson
Publishing Assistant: Claire Morgan
Designer: Fiona Grant
Series Consultant: Dee Reid

Photos: Cover image: Cultura/REX
Page 5: Inmagine/Alamy
Page 6: © John_ Woodcock/iStock
Page 7: Action Press/REX
Page 8: Image Broker/Robert Harding
Page 9: Sipa Press/REX
Page 10: Design Pics Inc/REX
Page 11: Cultura/REX
Page 12: © The Art Archive/Alamy
Page 14: © The National Trust Photolibrary/Alamy
Page 15: Universal History Archive/Un/REX
Page 16: Design Pics Inc/REX
Page 18: Design Pics Inc/REX
Page 19: Eric Vidal/REX
Page 20: Jonathon Browning/REX
Page 21: Top Photo Group/REX
Page 22: © RIA Novosti/Alamy
Page 24: Image Broker/REX
Page 25: © Alistair Flack/Alamy
Page 26: Zuma/REX
Page 27: Zuma/REX
Page 28: Wang Yuguo/REX
Page 29: Wang Lili/REX
Page 30: © Blend Images/Alamy

Attempts to contact all copyright holders have been made.
If any omitted would care to contact Badger Learning, we will be happy to make appropriate arrangements.

Contents

Vocabulary

empress   polar region

equipment   sculpture

hailstone   temperature

iceberg   thatched

1. What is ice?

On a hot day, do you like to have a cool drink with ice?

It's easy to make ice cubes.

Just put water in a mould and freeze it.

After three hours the water will have frozen into solid ice.

But there is a lot more to ice than just cooling a drink.

On Earth, ice forms on land and water where the temperature is below freezing.

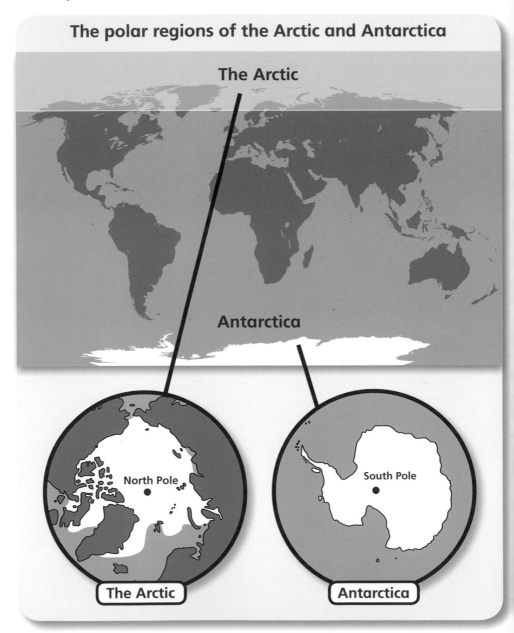

The polar regions of the Arctic and Antarctica

The Arctic

Antarctica

North Pole

South Pole

The Arctic

Antarctica

The polar regions are covered in huge areas of ice, called ice sheets. These have been formed by tons of packed down snow.

Sea ice is frozen seawater.

Icebreaker ships have powerful engines and special hulls to help them move through the ice.

Hailstones

When it is very cold, rain can turn into hard balls of ice, called hailstones. They can cause a lot of damage to vehicles, buildings and crops.

WOW! facts

The heaviest hailstone on record was one kilogram – the same weight as a bag of sugar!

Ice storm!

When freezing rain hits very cold ground, it turns into ice. Everything is covered in a smooth layer of thick ice.

Dangers of an ice storm:
- slippery ice on the roads and pavements
- tree branches breaking
- power lines falling over

2. Floating ice monsters – icebergs

Icebergs are huge pieces of ice that float in the ocean. An iceberg can be massive. The ice above water is only the top part – most of the iceberg is below the surface.

Icebergs slowly float on the ocean currents.

As they float into warmer water, most icebergs break up into smaller bits and then disappear.

However, sometimes big icebergs float into parts of the sea where there are lots of ships. This can be very dangerous.

On April 15 1912, the RMS Titanic hit an iceberg off the coast of Newfoundland. This is what the newspapers said:

Daily Newspaper

TUESDAY 16TH APRIL 1912

TITANIC HITS ICEBERG

Yesterday, the RMS Titanic hit a huge iceberg and sank. Over 1500 are feared to have drowned.

The Titanic was on its way from Liverpool to New York when disaster struck. All that is left of the ship is wreckage floating on the North Atlantic Ocean.

How big was the iceberg?

- The iceberg was 30.4 metres high – about the height of a ten-storey building.

- The iceberg was between 60.9 metres and 121.9 metres wide – more than the length of three football pitches.

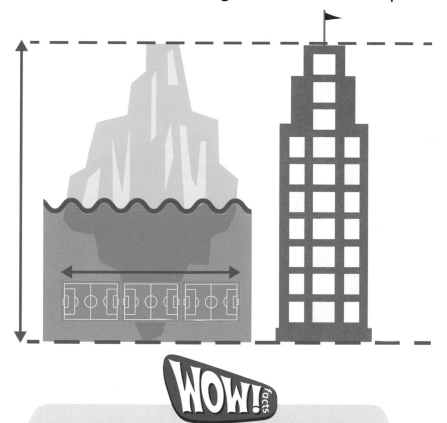

The International Ice Patrol now warns ships of icebergs in the North Atlantic Ocean.

3. The ice trade

In the past, people did not have fridges or freezers to keep their food fresh.

However, from the 1600s, rich people began to build ice houses in their gardens.

In the winter they would collect huge blocks of ice from frozen rivers and then pack the ice around the food.

Inside the ice house was an underground pit lined with bricks. This kept the ice as cold as possible. The thatched roof also helped to keep heat out.

WOW! facts

Old ice houses were sometimes used as air raid shelters during the Second World War.

Soon, more and more people wanted ice to keep their food fresh in the summer.

In the 19th Century, one man made it his business to get ice to people. He was an American called Frederic Tudor.

At first Frederic made no money because the ice melted too quickly.

Then he used an ice cutting machine pulled by horses. Now Frederic could get the ice much quicker. He loaded the ice into ships packed with sawdust and sent it from the United States to places like Great Britain and India. He became known as the 'Ice King.'

How ice was sent to Great Britain:

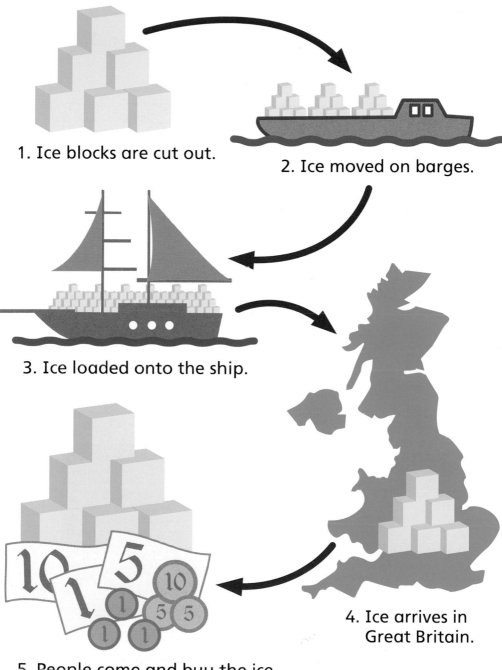

1. Ice blocks are cut out.

2. Ice moved on barges.

3. Ice loaded onto the ship.

4. Ice arrives in Great Britain.

5. People come and buy the ice.

Ice can be carved into sculptures of all shapes and sizes.

Small ice sculptures are often used as decorations for special events.

The sculptor has to work quickly before the ice melts.

Some ice sculptors use a chisel but some ice sculptors use a chainsaw to shape the sculpture.

It's quite tricky to cut the ice quickly with a chainsaw without cutting off your finger!

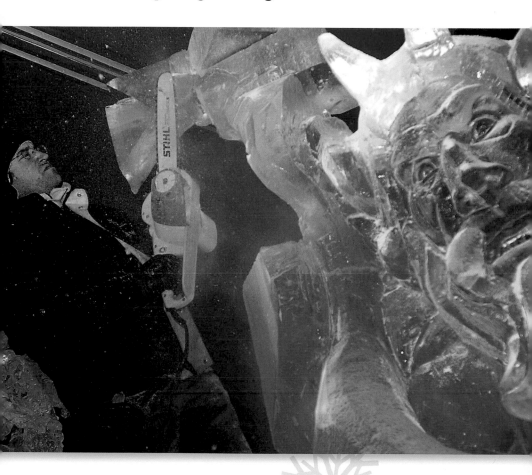

Every winter, thousands of people like to visit the Ice and Snow Sculpture Festival in northeast China.

Because the temperatures are freezing, the huge ice buildings and sculptures that are built can last for many weeks.

Different coloured lights make the ice look amazing at night.

5. Ice buildings

Ice palaces

In 1739, Empress Anna Ivanovna of Russia built an ice palace in Saint Petersburg.

Everything was made from ice, including the doors, furniture and pillows. Even the garden had ice birds sitting in ice trees!

The empress never lived in the palace but she did use it to punish two workers who had disobeyed her.

Diary of Empress Anna Ivanovna

Yesterday two workers were taken to the ice palace.

Once they got there, they were stripped and locked in a room. We thought that they would freeze to death, but this morning they came out alive!

It turns out a guard had given them a sheepskin rug.

In the James Bond film *Die Another Day*, the main villain has a huge ice palace in Iceland.

Ice hotels

During the winter, people can travel to places within the Arctic Circle to stay in ice hotels.

Even the hotel furniture – such as the chairs, lights and beds – is made of ice. As ice is so cold, the guests have to dress up warmly when they go to bed! Brrr!

WOW! facts

In Antarctica, ships can dock by piers made from ice.

Ice can also be used for sport.

Sport: Ice dancing

What it is: dancing on ice to set movements

Where: large indoor or outdoor ice rink

Equipment: ice skates
and costume

Sport: Speed skating

What it is: racing against other competitors on a track

Where: indoor or outdoor arena

Equipment: speed skates, spandex suit, protective headgear, gloves and eyewear

Sport: Ice curling

What it is: two teams slide a smooth stone along an ice lane towards a round target area. Brooms sweep the ice to help the stone move.

Where: inside arena

Equipment: eight stones, curling lane, brooms

Sport: Ice hockey

What it is: two teams of players use hockey sticks to shoot a puck into the other team's net

Where: indoor arena

Equipment: hockey stick, puck, skates, protective body gear

WOW! facts

The fastest ice hockey shot in the world was 110 miles per hour

Ice climbing

For ice climbers, ice can offer them a dangerous and exciting extreme sport.

Using just ice picks, ropes and spiked climbing boots, ice climbers climb up frozen waterfalls or the steep sides of glaciers.

So next time you make ice cubes, remember just how amazing ice can be.

Questions

What are hailstones? *(page 8)*

When did the Titanic sink? *(page 12)*

What were the first freezers called? *(page 14)*

What was Frederic Tudor's nickname? *(page 16)*

Name a tool used by ice sculptors. *(page 19)*

Name a piece of equipment needed for ice hockey. *(page 29)*

Index